DIG DEEP!

Bugs That Live
Underground

T000480

Trap-Door Spiders

Emily Wilson

PowerKiDS
press.

New York

Published in 2017 by The Rosen Publishing Group, Inc.
29 East 21st Street, New York, NY 10010

First Edition

Editor: Sarah Machajewski
Book Design: Mickey Harmon

Photo Credits: Cover (sky) Severe/Shutterstock.com; cover (background) ifong/Shutterstock.com; cover (trap-door spider) zstock/Shutterstock.com; pp. 3–4, 6, 8, 10, 12, 14, 16, 18, 20, 22–24 (background) isaravut/Shutterstock.com; p. 5 Dr Paul A Zahl/Science Source/Getty Images; p. 6 Melinda Fawver/Shutterstock.com; pp. 7, 13 James H Robinson/Science Source/Getty Images; p. 9 Auscape/UIG/Universal Images Group/Getty Images; p. 11 N A S. -/Science Source/Getty Images; p. 15 Simon D Pollard/Science Source/Getty Images; p. 17 kurt_G/Shutterstock.com; p. 19 © FLPA/Alamy Stock Photo; p. 21 Paul Zahl/Contributor/National Geographic/Getty Images; p. 22 Matteo photos/Shutterstock.com.

Cataloging-in-Publication Data

Names: Wilson, Emily.
Title: Trap-door spiders / Emily Wilson.
Description: New York : PowerKids Press, 2017. | Series: Dig deep! bugs that live underground | Includes index.
Identifiers: ISBN 9781499420661 (pbk.) | ISBN 9781499420685 (library bound) | ISBN 9781499420678 (6 pack)
Subjects: LCSH: Trap-door spiders–Juvenile literature.
Classification: LCC QL458.4 W554 2017 | DDC 595.4'4–d23

Manufactured in the United States of America

CPSIA Compliance Information: Batch #BS16PK: For Further Information contact Rosen Publishing, New York, New York at 1-800-237-9932

Contents

Predatory Practices

Animals have developed cool ways of catching food. Cheetahs run at top speeds to catch their **prey**. Frogs use their long, sticky tongue to catch flies out of the air. Some snakes squeeze their prey to death.

Spiders are known for **weaving** webs to trap **insects**. The trap-door spider does things a little differently. It builds a burrow in the ground and waits behind a door made of silk. When its prey walks by, the trap-door spider jumps out and grabs it! It may sound gross, but this practiced predator is fascinating. Let's dig deep into the life of a trap-door spider.

Watch out for the trap-door spider—it's sneaky!

Spider Families

Most trap-door spiders belong to a family of spiders called ctenizidae. They are called ctenizids. However, there are also trap-door spiders in a number of other spider families.

In the United States, ctenizids live in the Southwest and on the Pacific coast, as well as in Florida, Alabama, Georgia, and North Carolina. They also live in other locations in China, North America, South America, Africa, Australia, and Japan. Trap-door spiders may live in other places, but we might not know it—they're great at hiding!

Dig Deeper!

One kind of trap-door spider lives around the world. Long ago, this species, or kind, may have moved across continents and settled in different places.

Scientists think there are around 120 species of trap-door spiders.

Spotting a Spider

Trap-door spiders are medium-sized. Their body is about 1 inch (2.5 cm) long, but it can be as long as 1.6 inches (4 cm). Trap-door spiders have an **abdomen** and a **thorax**. Their body is covered with tiny hairs.

Trap-door spiders have eight thick, short legs. They also have eight eyes. Some species have a pair of eyes in the middle of their head and three eyes on each side. Ctenizid trap-door spiders have a row of teeth that are made for digging. This helps them create their burrow. They also have fangs that they use to stab into their prey.

Dig Deeper!

Trap-door spiders are usually dull brown, but they can also be yellowish brown, reddish brown, and black.

thorax

abdomen

Trap-door spiders may look scary, but they aren't harmful to humans.

Making a Burrow

Most species of trap-door spiders construct, or build, an underground nest called a burrow. Burrows are tunnels that can be up to 6 inches (15.2 cm) long. Some burrows are just one tunnel, while others have tunnels branching off from the main one. Trap-door spiders generally stay in their burrow unless they're hunting or looking for a **mate**.

Trap-door spiders cover the entrance to their nest with a door made of soil, plants, and silk. These materials **camouflage** the door, which allows the spider to surprise its prey. The trapdoor has a **hinge** on one side that allows it to open and close.

Dig Deeper!

Despite their name, not all trap-door spiders make a door for their burrow.

The door to this burrow blends in so well with its surroundings that it's hard to see. That's good for the spider, but not for its prey.

Lying in Wait

Trap-door spiders wait inside their burrow until a meal walks by. The spiders hold the underside of the door with claws attached to their first set of legs. They can't see their prey coming, but they can feel it.

Some spiders lay lines of silk around their burrow. When a bug walks over the lines, the silk **vibrates**, telling the spider a meal is nearby. As soon as spiders **detect** their prey, they leap out of their burrow and grab it! If a trap-door spider is really hungry, it will wait for prey with half its body outside the nest.

Trap-door spiders act fast! They have to if they want to eat.

Killer!

Trap-door spiders hide until they can surprise their prey. What do they prey on? Trap-door spiders eat all kinds of bugs. They're also known to eat mice, frogs, young snakes, and baby birds. Some trap-door spiders create burrows near water so they can catch small fish.

Once its prey is close enough, the trap-door spider comes out of its burrow and raises its body on its back legs. Then, the spider strikes, biting its prey with its sharp fangs. The fangs release a fast-acting venom, or poison, which kills the prey. The trap-door spider then drags the unlucky bug back to its burrow.

The trap-door spider's sharp fangs can bite through a bug's hard body.

fangs

Hunted

While trap-door spiders are sneaky hunters, they're hunted, too. They have many predators. Birds, centipedes, scorpions, wasps, and flies prey on the trap-door spider. Parasitic wasps, such as spider wasps, are one of their worst enemies.

Female spider wasps prey on spiders because they lay their eggs on the spider's body. When the wasp finds the spider's burrow, it sneaks in to sting the spider. The sting paralyzes the spider, which means it can't move. Then, the female lays an egg on the spider's abdomen. When the egg hatches, the young wasp eats the spider. It's still alive!

Dig Deeper!

A parasite is an **organism** that lives in or on another organism. "Parasitic" is a word used to describe parasites.

A trap-door spider can try to hide in its burrow to escape a wasp, but the wasp usually wins. It can cut through the trapdoor with its fangs.

The Spider Life Cycle

Trap-door spiders help their species survive by reproducing. That means they make baby trap-door spiders. While female spiders usually stick close to their burrow, adult males leave theirs in search of a mate.

Female trap-door spiders lay their eggs inside their burrow. There, the eggs are protected from predators and other harm in the outside world. A few months after the spiders mate, the eggs hatch into tiny spiders called spiderlings. The female trap-door spider feeds the spiderlings inside the burrow. She feeds them food that she ate and threw up!

A spiderling looks a lot like an adult spider—only smaller!

On Their Own

Trap-door spiderlings stay in the nest for several months. They then leave to make their own burrows. A spiderling's burrow is small at first, to match its size. However, as the spider grows, it makes the burrow bigger. Species that build trapdoors also have to make the trapdoor bigger. Trapdoors that haven't been harmed show the rings of silk that were added as the spider grew up.

It takes many years for these spiders to be fully grown. Adult trap-door spiders can live from five to 20 years. Hiding underground, away from danger, may be the key to living a long life!

Dig Deeper!

Some people keep trap-door spiders as pets.

The trap-door spider's underground burrow is important to its survival.

Pretty Harmless

Trap-door spiders are big and hairy. They use sneak attacks when hunting their prey. They live underground, and we might not even know they're there! All these things may make the trap-door spider seem scary, but there's no reason to be afraid. Actually, they're probably more afraid of us than we are of them. If the trap-door spider senses danger, it will run away and hide. That isn't so bad!

Even though trap-door spiders are generally harmless, it's important to be careful around them. They can bite people, and their bite can hurt. If you see a trap-door spider, leave it alone. It's the best thing for you—and the spider.

Glossary

abdomen: The rear section of a spider's body.

camouflage: To hide or cause something to blend in with its surroundings.

detect: To feel the presence of something.

hinge: A part that connects two objects and allows them to move.

insect: A bug that has six legs and one or two pairs of wings.

mate: Each of a pair of animals or bugs that come together to make babies. Also, to come together to make babies.

organism: A living thing.

prey: To hunt another animal for food. Also, an animal that's hunted by another animal for food.

thorax: The front section of a spider's body that includes the head and legs.

weave: To make something from connected threads.

vibrate: To move rapidly back and forth.

Index

Websites

Due to the changing nature of Internet links, PowerKids Press has developed an online list of websites related to the subject of this book. This site is updated regularly. Please use this link to access the list: www.powerkidslinks.com/digd/trap